Advent Antiphons

Bob Chilcott

for SATB double choir a cappella

Vocal score

MUSIC DEPARTMENT

OXFORD
UNIVERSITY PRESS

OXFORD
UNIVERSITY PRESS

Great Clarendon Street, Oxford OX2 6DP, England
198 Madison Avenue, New York, NY10016, USA

Oxford University Press is a department of the University of Oxford.
It furthers the University's aim of excellence in research, scholarship,
and education by publishing worldwide in

Oxford New York
Auckland Bangkok Buenos Aires Cape Town Chennai
Dar es Salaam Delhi Hong Kong Istanbul Karachi Kolkata
Kuala Lumpur Madrid Melbourne Mexico City Mumbai Nairobi
São Paulo Shanghai Taipei Tokyo Toronto

Oxford is a registered trade mark of Oxford University Press
in the UK and in certain other countries

First published 2005

11

ISBN 0-19-343336-2

Music and text origination by
Barnes Music Engraving Ltd., East Sussex
Printed in Great Britain on acid-free paper by
Halstan & Co. Ltd., Amersham, Bucks.

Contents

Composer's note

The texts for this piece are known as the 'Great O Antiphons'. They anticipate the coming of Christmas, and were traditionally sung before and after the Magnificat on the seven days preceding Christmas Eve. They will be familiar to many in their paraphrased version in the hymn 'Veni, veni, Emmanuel' ('O come, O come, Emmanuel'). When the first letters of the antiphons are read backwards we read the acrostic 'ero cras' – 'tomorrow I will be with you'.

The music is based on the plainsong melody, and at the beginning of each 'O' the beginning of the melody is heard, either unison or harmonized.

I wrote this piece for the Cathedral Choir in Reykjavik, and we performed it there for the first time at the end of October 2004.

English translation of texts

O wisdom, coming forth from the Most High, filling all creation and reigning to the ends of the earth: come and teach us the way of truth.

O Lord of Lords, and ruler of the House of Israel, you appeared to Moses in the fire of the burning bush, and gave him the law on Sinai: come with your outstretched arm and ransom us.

O root of Jesse, standing as a sign among the nations; kings will keep silence before you for whom the nations long: come and save us and delay no longer.

O key of David and sceptre of the House of Israel; you open and none can shut; you shut and none can open: come and free the captives from prison, and break down the walls of death.

O morning star, splendour of the light eternal and bright sun of righteousness: come and bring light to those who dwell in darkness and walk in the shadow of death.

O king of the nations, you alone can fulfil their desire; cornerstone, binding all together: come and save the creature you fashioned from the dust of the earth.

O Emmanuel, our King and Lawgiver, hope of the nations and their saviour: come and save us, O Lord our God.

Duration: *c.*10 minutes

Composed for the Reykjavik Cathedral Choir's 24th Annual 'Solo Dei Gloria' Festival, 2004

Advent Antiphons

The Great O Antiphons
Rite of Salisbury

BOB CHILCOTT

1. *O Sapientia*

Printed in Great Britain

OXFORD UNIVERSITY PRESS, MUSIC DEPARTMENT, GREAT CLARENDON STREET, OXFORD OX2 6DP

6
mp
Sa - pi - en - ti - a, O___ Sa - pi - en - ti - a,___ Sa-pi - en-ti - a,__
Sa - pi - en - ti - a, O Sa - pi - en - ti - a,___ Sa-pi - en-ti - a,__
Sa - pi - en - ti - a, O Sa - pi - en - ti - a,___ Sa-pi - en-ti - a,__
Sa - pi - en - ti - a, O___ Sa - pi - en - ti - a,___ Sa-pi - en-ti - a,__
p espress.
O Sa-pi - en - ti - a,___
O Sa-pi - en - ti - a,___
O Sa-pi - en - ti - a,___
O Sa-pi - en - ti - a,___

14
p
mp
mf
quae ex o - re Al - tis - si -
quae ex o - re Al -
quae ex o - re
quae ex
p cresc.
quae ex o - re Al - tis - si - mi pro - di -
quae ex o - re Al - tis - si - mi pro - di -
quae ex o - re, o - re Al - tis - si - mi pro - di -
quae ex o - re Al - tis - si - mi pro -

21
dim.
pp
-mi pro-di-sti, at - tin -
-tis-si-mi pro - di - sti, at - tin -
Al - tis-si-mi pro - di - sti, at - tin -
o - re Al-tis-si - mi pro-di - sti, at - tin -
p
-sti, pro - di - sti, at - tin - gens a
-sti, pro - - di - sti, at - tin - gens a
-sti, pro - di - sti, at - tin - gens a
- di - sti, pro-di-sti, at - tin - gens a

27
mp cresc.
f espress.
- gens, ad fi - nem for - ti - ter: su -
- gens, ad fi - nem for - ti - ter: su -
- gens, ad fi - nem for - ti - ter: su -
- gens, ad fi - nem for - ti - ter: su -
cresc.
f espress.
fi - ne us - que ad fi - nem for - ti - ter: su - a - vi -
fi - ne us - que ad fi - nem for - ti - ter: su - a - vi -
fi - ne us - que ad fi - nem for - ti - ter: su - a - vi -
fi - ne us - que ad fi - nem for - ti - ter: su - a - vi -
cresc.
f

34
poco rit.
a tempo
p
-a - vi - ter dis - po-nens-que om - ni - a: Ve - ni,
p
-a - vi - ter dis - po-nens-que om - ni - a: Ve - ni,
p
-a - vi - ter dis - po-nens-que om - ni - a: Ve - ni,
p
-a - vi - ter dis - po-nens-que om - ni - a: Ve - ni,
-ter dis - po - nens - que om - ni - a:
-ter dis - po-nens - que om - ni - a:
-ter dis - po-nens - que om - ni - a:
-ter dis - po-nens - que om - ni - a:
poco rit.
a tempo
p

41
poco rit.
a little slower
mp
p
ve - ni, ad do - cen - dum nos vi - am pru - den - ti - ae.
ve - ni, ad do - cen - dum nos vi - am pru - den - ti - ae.
ve - ni, ad do - cen - dum nos vi - am pru - den - ti - ae.
ve - ni, ad do - cen - dum nos vi - am pru - den - ti - ae.
poco rit.
a little slower
mp
p

2. O Adonaï

a tempo
48
p espress.
O A - do - na - ï,
O A - do - na - ï,
O A - do - na - ï,
O A - do - na - ï,
O
O A - do - na - ï, O
O A - do - na - ï, O
O A - do - na - ï, O
a tempo
p espress.

52
p
p
O A - do - na - ï,
O A - do - na - ï,
O A - do - na - ï,
O A - do - na - ï,
A - do - na - ï, O A - do - na -
A - do - na - ï, O A - do - na -
A - do - na - ï, O A - do - na -
A - do - na - ï, O A - do - na -

56
mp
p cresc.
O A - do - na - ï,
O A - do - na - ï,
- ï,
et dux do - mus Is - ra - el,
mp cresc.
qui
cresc.

59
mf
A - do - na - ï,
mf
A - do - na - ï,
mf
A - do - na - ï,
mf
A - do - na - ï,
Mo - ï - si in ig - ne flam - me ru - bi ap - pa - ru -
mp cresc.
qui, qui Mo - ï - si in ig - ne flam - me ru - bi ap -
mp cresc.
qui, qui Mo - ï - si in ig - ne flam - me ru - bi ap -
mp cresc.
qui, qui Mo - ï - si in ig - ne flam - me ru - bi ap -
mp cresc.

64
mf
f
O A - do - na - ï, A - do - na - ï,
O A - do - na - ï, A - do - na - ï,
O A - do - na - ï, A - do - na - ï,
O A - do - na - ï, A - do - na - ï,
f cresc.
dim.
- i - sti, et e - i in Sy - na le - gem
- pa - ru - i - sti, et e - i in Sy - na le - gem
- pa - ru - i - sti, et e - i in Sy - na le - gem
- pa - ru - i - sti, et e - i in Sy - na le - gem
f
dim.

poco rit.
a tempo
68
mp
p
O A-do-na-ï, O A-do-na-ï, A-
de-di-sti: Ve-ni, ve-ni ad
poco rit.
a tempo

a little slower
poco rit.
72
-do - na - ï,
-do - na - ï,
-do - na - ï,
-do - na - ï,
pp
re - di - men - dum nos in bra - chi - o ex - ten - to.
re - di - men - dum nos in bra - chi - o ex - ten - to.
re - di - men - dum nos in bra - chi - o ex - ten - to.
re - di - men - dum nos in bra - chi - o ex - ten - to.
a little slower
poco rit.
pp

3. *O Radix Jesse*

80
poco cresc.
O Ra - dix Jes - se,
poco cresc.
O Ra - dix Jes - se,
poco cresc.
sig - num po - pu - lo - rum, su - per quem re - ges con - ti - ne - bunt
poco cresc.
sig - num po - pu - lo - rum, su - per quem re - ges con - ti - ne - bunt
poco cresc.
O Ra - dix Jes - se,
poco cresc.
O Ra - dix Jes - se,
poco cresc.
sig - num po - pu - lo - rum, su - per quem re - ges con - ti - ne - bunt
poco cresc.
O
poco cresc.

85
mf
Ra - dix Jes - se,
mf
Ra - dix Jes - se,
mf espress.
os - su - um, quem gen - tes de -
mf espress.
os - su - um, quem gen - tes de -
mf
Ra - dix Jes - se, Ra -
mf
Ra - dix Jes - se, Ra -
mf espress.
os - su - um, quem gen - tes
mf
O
mf

90
(fade)
Ra - - dix, Ra - dix,
(fade)
Ra - dix, Ra - dix Jes - se,
- pre - ca - bun - tur:
- pre - ca - bun - tur:
(fade)
- - dix, Ra - dix,
(fade)
- dix, Ra - dix Jes - se,
de - pre - ca - bun - tur:
O

93
pp
O Ra - dix Jes - -
pp
O Ra - dix Jes -
Ve - ni, ve - ni ad li - be -
Ve - ni, ve - ni ad li - be -
pp
O Ra - dix Jes -
pp
O Ra - dix Jes -
Ve - ni, ve - ni ad li - be -
Ve - ni, ve - ni ad li - be -

95
(fade)
rit.
- se,
(fade)
- se,
pp
- ran - dum nos, jam no - li tar - da - re.
pp
- ran - dum nos, jam no - li tar - da - re.
(fade)
- se,
(fade)
- se,
pp
- ran - dum nos, jam no - li tar - da - re.
pp
- ran - dum nos, jam no - li tar - da - re.
rit.
pp

4. *O Clavis David*

103
S.
A.
T.
B.
et sce - ptrum do - mus Is - ra - el,
O Cla - vis Da - vid, Cla - vis, Cla - vis Da - vid,
O Cla - vis Da -
S.
A.
T.
B.
et sce - ptrum do - mus Is - ra -
O Cla - vis Da - vid, Da - vid, O
O Cla - vis Da -

108
mp cresc.
— qui a - pe - ris et ne - mo clau - dit,
mp cresc.
qui a - pe - ris et ne - mo clau - dit,
cresc.
mp cresc.
— Da - vid, qui a - pe - ris et ne - mo
cresc.
mp cresc.
- vid, Da - vid, qui a - pe - ris et ne - mo
mp cresc.
- el, qui a - pe - ris et ne - mo clau - dit,
mp cresc.
qui a - pe - ris et ne - mo clau - dit,
cresc.
mp cresc.
Cla - vis Da - vid, qui a - pe - ris et ne - mo
cresc.
- vid, qui a - pe - ris,
cresc.

113
f
dim.
rit.
p
clau - dis et ne - mo a - pe - rit:
clau - dis et ne - mo a - pe - rit:
clau - dit, clau - dis et ne - mo a - pe - rit:
clau - dit, et ne - mo a - pe - rit:
clau - dis et ne - mo a - pe - rit:
clau - dis et ne - mo a - pe - rit:
clau - dit, et ne - mo a - pe - rit:
clau - dis et ne - mo a - pe - rit:

119
a tempo
p
S.1
Ve - ni, ve - ni,
S.2
Ve - ni, ve - ni,
A.
Ve - ni, ve - ni,
T.
Ve - ni, ve - ni,
B.
Ve - ni, ve - ni,
S.
Ve - ni, ve - ni,
A.
Ve - ni, ve - ni,
T.
Ve - ni, ve - ni,
B.
Ve - ni, ve - ni,
a tempo

123
S.
A.
T.
et e - duc vin - ctum, vin - ctum de
B.
Ve - ni, ve - ni, de
S.
A.
T.
et e - duc vin - ctum de
B.
Ve - - ni, de

128
pp
se - den - tem in
pp
O Cla -
pp
do - mo car - ce - ris,
O Cla -
pp
do - mo car - ce - ris,
se - den - tem in
pp
se - den - tem in
pp
do - mo car - ce - ris,
O Cla -
pp
do - mo car - ce - ris,
O Cla -
pp

132
rit.
te - ne - bris et um - bra mor - tis.
-vis Da - vid, et um - bra mor - tis.
-vis Da - vid, et um - bra mor - tis.
te - ne - bris
te - ne - bris et um - bra mor - tis.
-vis Da - vid,
-vis Da - vid,
rit.

(for Andrew Potter)

5. O Oriens

142
(each singer sing phrases independently and in own rhythm)
p
splen - dor lu - cis,
O - - ri - ens, O O - - ri -
mp
splen-dor lu - cis ae - ter - nae,
mp
splen-dor lu - cis ae - ter - nae,
(each singer sing phrases independently and in own rhythm)
p
splen - dor lu - cis,
- - ri - ens, O O - - ri - ens,
mp
splen-dor lu - cis ae -
mp
splen-dor lu - cis ae -
mp

148
mp
ae - ter - -
mp
- ens,
O O -
mf
et sol ju - sti - ti - ae:
Ve -
mf
et sol ju - sti - ti - ae:
Ve -
mp
ae - ter - - nae,
mp
O O - ri - ens,
mf
- ter - nae, et sol ju - sti - ti - ae:
Ve -
mf
- ter - nae, et sol ju - sti - ti - ae:
Ve -
mf

156
(fade)
p
-nae,
O___ O - ri - ens,
(fade)
p
-ri - ens,
O___ O - ri - ens,
mp
-ni, ve - ni, ve - ni,
mp
-ni,___ ve - ni, ve - ni,
(fade)
p
O___ O - ri - ens,
(fade)
p
O___ O - ri - ens,
mp
-ni, ve - ni, ve - ni,
mp
-ni,___ ve - ni, ve - ni,
mp

164
mp espress.
Ve - ni, et il -
p
splen - dor lu - cis,
p
O O - ri - ens,
p
O
mp espress.
Ve - ni, et il -
p
splen - dor lu - cis,
p
O O - ri - ens,
p
O
mp

171
-lu - mi - na se - den - tem in te - ne - bris
- cis,
- ens,
O - ri - ens,
-lu - mi - na se - den - tem in te - ne - bris
- cis,
- ens,
O - ri - ens,

a little slower
176
p
et um - bra mor - tis.
p
et um - bra mor - tis.
a little slower
p

6. *O Rex gentium*

184
dim.
p cresc.
et de - si - de - ra - tus e - a - rum: O Rex
et de - si - de - ra - tus e - a - rum: O Rex
et de - si - de - ra - tus e - a - rum: O Rex
et de - si - de - ra - tus e - a - rum: O Rex
p cresc.
- ra - tus e - a - rum: La - pis - que an - gu -
- ra - tus e - a - rum: La - pis - que an - gu -
- ra - tus e - a - rum: La - pis - que an - gu -
- ra - tus e - a - rum: La - pis - que an - gu -
dim.
p cresc.

189
mf cresc.
ff
gen - ti-um, O Rex gen - ti - um, Ve -
gen - ti-um, O Rex gen - ti - um, Ve -
gen - ti-um, O Rex gen - ti - um, Ve -
gen - ti-um, O Rex gen - ti - um, Ve -
-la - ris, qui fa - cis u-tra-que u - num, Ve - ni,
-la - ris, qui fa - cis u-tra-que u - num, Ve - ni,
-la - ris, qui fa - cis u-tra-que u - num, Ve - ni,
-la - ris, qui fa - cis u-tra-que u - num, Ve - ni,

rit.
Tempo I (♩ = c.96)
196
p
-ni, sal - va ho - mi - nem, Ve - ni, ve -
-ni, sal - va ho - mi - nem, Ve - ni, ve -
-ni, sal - va ho - mi - nem, Ve - ni, ve -
-ni, sal - va ho - mi - nem, Ve - ni, ve -
sal - va ho - mi - nem,
sal - va ho - mi - nem,
sal - va ho - mi - nem,
sal - va ho - mi - nem,
rit.
Tempo I (♩ = c.96)
p

203
rit.
a tempo
rit.
mp
p
- ni, sal - va ho - mi - nem, quem de li - mo for - mas - ti.
- ni, sal - va ho - mi - nem, quem de li - mo for - mas - ti.
- ni, sal - va ho - mi - nem, quem de li - mo for - mas - ti.
- ni, sal - va ho - mi - nem, quem de li - mo for - mas - ti.
rit.
a tempo
rit.
mp
p

7. O Emmanuel

a tempo
210
p espress.
O Em - ma - nu - el,
p espress.
O Em - ma - nu - el,
p espress.
O Em - ma - nu - el, Rex et Le - gi - fer
p espress.
O Em - ma - nu - el, Rex et Le - gi - fer
p espress.
O Em - ma - nu - el,
p espress.
O Em - ma - nu - el,
p espress.
O Em - ma - nu - el,
a tempo
p espress.

215
mp
mf
ex-pec - ta - ti - o gen - ti - um
nos - ter, ex-pec - ta - ti - o gen - ti - um et Sal -
ex-pec - ta - ti - o gen - ti - um

221
mf
f
Ve - ni, ve - ni,
Ve - ni, ve - ni,
-va - tor e - a - rum: Ve - ni, ve - ni, ad sal -
-va - tor e - a - rum: Ve - ni, ve - ni, ad sal -
Ve - ni, ve - ni,
Ve - ni, ve - ni,
Ve - ni, ve - ni,
Ve - ni, ve - ni,

226
ff
mf
Do - mi - ne
De - us
-van - dum nos
Do - mi - ne
De - us no - ster,

232
mp
p
no - ster,
De - us
no - ster,
De - us
no - ster.
dim.